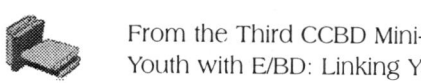 From the Third CCBD Mini-L
Youth with E/BD: Linking Ye

MW01594952

Educating Students with Emotional and Behavioral Disorders

Historical Perspective and Future Directions

Richard J. Whelan
The University of Kansas
Medical Center

James M. Kauffman
University of Virginia

Lyndal M. Bullock & Robert A. Gable, *Series Editors*

Council for Children with Behavioral Disorders

The Council for Children with Behavioral Disorders, *Publisher*

About the Council for Children with Behavioral Disorders

Council for
Children with
Behavioral
Disorders

CCBD is an international and professional organization committed to promoting and facilitating the education and general welfare of children and youth with behavioral and emotional disorders. CCBD, whose members include educators, parents, mental health personnel, and a variety of other professionals, actively pursues quality educational services and program alternatives for persons with behavioral disorders, advocates for the needs of such children and youth, emphasizes research and professional growth as vehicles for better understanding behavioral disorders, and provides professional support for persons who are involved with and serve children and youth with behavioral disorders.

In advocating for the professionals in the field of behavioral disorders, CCBD (a division of The Council for Exceptional Children) endorses the Standards for Professional Practice and Code of Ethics adopted by the Delegate Assembly of The Council for Exceptional Children in 1983.

Stock No. D5329, ISBN 0-86586-352-0

Copyright © 1999 by the Council for Children with Behavioral Disorders, a Division of The Council for Exceptional Children, 1920 Association Drive, Reston, Virginia 20191-1589.

Printed in the United States of America

10   9   8   7   6   5   4   3   2   1

Contents

Foreword

Public education is in transition. Pressure is mounting to establish and maintain safe and effective schools—schools that produce positive educational outcomes for all students. Recent federal legislation has prompted the redefinition of roles and responsibilities of many school personnel, especially those working with students who have disabilities or are at risk. In serving students labeled "seriously emotionally disturbed," "behaviorally disordered," or "emotionally/behaviorally disordered," we face new challenges to promoting positive approaches to discipline and instruction within and across educational settings.

In the midst of these uncertain times, we would do well to reflect on our history, revisit the theoretical underpinnings of our profession, and renew our commitment to finding ways to better serve students with emotional and behavioral disorders. That is the focus of the Third Mini-Library Series produced by the Council for Children with Behavioral Disorders (CCBD). Along with an exploration of historical and contemporary issues within our profession, this monograph series highlights the critical issues of safe schools, school-wide discipline, and positive behavioral supports. The following seven volumes that comprise the series are derived from the 1999 international conference sponsored by CCBD:

- *Developing Positive Behavioral Support for Students with Challenging Behaviors* by George Sugai and Timothy J. Lewis.

- *Educating Students with Emotional and Behavioral Disorders: Historical Perspective and Future Directions* by Richard J. Whelan and James M. Kauffman.

- *Historical Chronology of the Council for Children with Behavioral Disorders: 1964–1999* by Lyndal M. Bullock and Anthony L. "Tony" Menendez.

- *Perspective on Emotional/Behavioral Disorders: Assumptions and Their Implications for Education and Treatment* by C. Michael Nelson, Terrance M. Scott, and Lewis Polsgrove.

- *Psychoeducation: An Idea Whose Time Has Come* by Mary M. Wood, Larry K. Brendtro, Frank A. Fecser, and Polly Nichols.

- *A Revisitation of the Ecological Perspectives on Emotional/Behavioral Disorders: Underlying Assumptions and Implications for Education and Treatment* by Mary Lynn Cantrell, Robert P. Cantrell, Thomas G. Valore, James M. Jones, and Frank A. Fecser.

- *Safe Schools: School-Wide Discipline Practices* by Timothy J. Lewis and George Sugai.

As in previous monographs, we have drawn upon the expertise of CCBD members to assemble information that addresses the needs of professionals responsible for the education and treatment of students at risk and those who have emotional and behavioral disorders. We are grateful for their outstanding contributions to our field.

Lyndal M. Bullock
University of North Texas

Robert A. Gable
Old Dominion University

PART I

HISTORICAL PERSPECTIVE

Richard J. Whelan

Introduction

When confronted with the charge to write a historical perspective on the field of emotional and behavioral disorders (E/BD), my thoughts turned to my mother, who was a teacher in a one-room school located on the "Great American Desert," now known as the Great Plains. She was responsible for teaching 15 to 20 children in grades 1 through 8 to read, write, spell, cipher, and in, general, be good citizens. In the pictures of her and the students, I see a true pioneer woman about 5 feet 3 inches tall surrounded by boys and girls of all sizes, some reaching a height of 6 feet and weighing 180 pounds. All of the students clearly loved this woman because she was a good person and a superior teacher. The students helped with the daily chores of cleaning, stoking the stove, carrying out ashes, washing chalkboards, and all the rest of the jobs connected with running a school. My mother was a teacher, principal, manager, budget officer, substitute parent, and, best of all, a positive role model. She provided the students with everything they needed, but not everything they wanted. She was a successful teacher and had a list of successful graduates to prove it. They were, one and all, good citizens who made many positive contributions to their community, their state, and their nation.

As I began my studies to be a teacher, and for many years thereafter, I asked my mother "How did you do it?" She always smiled and said that "everybody helped everybody." The older ones helped the young ones; the fast young ones helped the slower older ones—peer-mediated instruction. When one group was being taught, another group practiced what they had learned—independent practice. Lessons were structured and individualized according to levels of performance—multiage grouping. There were projects to be done, especially dealing with problems of farming and ranching—cooperative and experiential learning. She had a structure to the lessons of the day, week, and month. It consisted of reviews, presenting new material, supervised practice in seat or at the board, feedback on performance, on-your-own-practice, and frequent reviews—effective instruction.

Shortly before my mother died, we had another conversation about her teaching days. I said, "You know Mom, you used what today is called *effective instruction*." She said something like "I am glad I was doing it right." I then asked, "Mom, where did you learn how to do all of this good teaching stuff?" After telling me that there are better words than "stuff," she shared her secret. "The students taught me; they let me know if I got it wrong or right. Their learning was my measure of failure or success." I said, "OK, but how about behavior problems?" Mom replied, "We were too busy for them most of the time, but *we* (students and teacher) developed a few simple rules to follow, like 'be respectful of others, ask permission, ask questions, work when you are supposed to, and play after work is completed.' This approach worked well. Also, the parents valued education and supported me 24 hours a day."

Here was a woman with a high school education—a very good one by the way, including two foreign languages—who attended two summer sessions on pedagogy sponsored by the county superintendent of education and practiced what today passes for educational reform. In fact, just a brief look at Table I.1 shows that my mother would be, as they say, "up to speed" today. This is also a great example to support the task of preserving memory banks; we learn so much from them. I do not propose my mother's experiences as a model for teacher education; there are too many unknowns. However, her commitment to instructional excellence, motivation to learn, sensitivity to diversity, and ability to self-evaluate is a model for entry into the profession.

When asked to address the following topics, I was transplanted back in time to my mother's experiences in teaching and also to a book titled *The University Can't Train Teachers* (Olson, Bowman, Free-

Table I.1
Instructional Practices
in the Old Days and Nowadays

Old Days	*Nowadays*
• Help each other	• Peer-mediated instruction
• Seat/chalkboard work	• Independent practice
• Structured lessons	• Presentation and guided practice
• Quick grading	• Corrections and feedback
• Project work	• Cooperative and experiential learning
• Frequent tests	• Systematic review

— — — — — — — — — — — — — —

BEST TEACHING PRACTICES	EFFECTIVE INSTRUCTION

man, & Pieper, 1972). The message in 1972 was that teacher education should be a university-wide responsibility, mostly centered in the schools where teachers teach, and that teacher education should be recognized as a critical topic for serious study in its own right. Parts of the message were received. Today, teacher education programs have established partnerships with professional development schools (PDSs).

The National Commission on Teaching and America's Future (1996) told us that teachers do not know subject matter, that they are not qualified in their field, and that 30% of them walk away from the classroom within 5 years. The universities that train teachers did not fare much better with the Commission, because about one half do not have accreditation from national professional agencies. Just a few years ago, similar committees were extolling the benefits of alternative certification based on life experience and a brief exposure to professional study. Which way will the winds of change blow in the next 5 years?

The foregoing is a rather lengthy run-up to the chapters that follow in Part I: 1. A Brief History; 2. People and Events; 3. Some Promising Practices; 4. Current Issues; and 5. Parting Comments. Keep in mind where children and youth with E/BD fit into the larger context of these topics. I will try to be clear, but I sure wish my mother were here to help with this piece of homework.

A Brief History 1

When I started work in the profession almost 50 years ago, 122 programs had sequences in one or more areas of exceptionality, and fewer than 14 had specialized work for teachers of children labeled as having E/BD (Mackie & Dunn, 1954). Teachers who wanted to work in the field held basic certification in elementary or secondary education, a few years of experience in general education, some training in psychopathology and its treatment, and motivation to make a difference in the lives of troubled and troublesome youth. These teachers had two choices for professional training. First, they could attend a university for a summer course of study that included a basic introduction to the education of exceptional children; specific characteristics of E/BD; methodology that usually included good developmental, corrective, or remedial procedures; some classroom management strategies reflective of the professor's philosophy; and, if fortunate, a brief supervised practicum with real children who displayed symptoms of E/BD. Or, second, the neophyte teacher could take a job in a well-managed residential or day school and be trained by professional staff, (e.g. psychiatrist, clinical psychologist, psychiatric social worker), experienced peer teachers, wise child-care workers, and the best of all trainers, the children. I used the second path and only later completed formalized preparation. It was not a bad choice.

Being a teacher was complicated somewhat because children with E/BD "belonged" to the mental health professionals who fixed them and then sent them back to school. How did teachers fit into that model? The best way was to be a *good teacher* and all that phrase means in terms of relationships and professional competence in the service of a Gestalt treatment strategy. If one taught within that strategy, then teaching and learning were therapeutic experiences. Education was the reality part of treatment, often a child's last contact with the world to be lost and the first to be regained. Teachers presented reality to their students to help reduce anxiety, but only the therapist was allowed to interpret the reality-based interactions. For example, teachers supported healthy defenses, whereas the therapist gave insight into them and how they related to the management of conflict. In short, teachers focused on strengthening a child's ego, and the therapist released the child from the tyranny of the id and superego.

This narrative is a simplified version of a complex context. In simple terms, the role of a teacher was to use a positive relationship to stimulate a child to learn until such time as the love of learning took over as intrinsic motivation to achieve. The process that I have described is what I was trained to do to help children with E/BD.

As school leaders recognized that children with E/BD were enrolled in their schools and that there would never be enough therapists or centers, they developed their own programs, mostly special classrooms. School-based programs were designed to accomplish two primary goals. The first goal was to change behaviors from maladaptive to adaptive and reinclude children in general education classrooms—a noble purpose. The second goal was to remove trouble, disruption, and general chaos from the general education classroom—also a noble purpose at that time, but not so much now, at least in the new "one size fits all" inclusion paradigm.

Where did the school leaders find teachers for this new group of exceptional children, a group that was not even counted in school surveys of the early 1950s (U.S. Department of Health, Education, and Welfare, 1954)? They transferred experienced teachers of students with mental retardation to E/BD classes, and they lobbied postsecondary institutions to start E/BD teacher education programs.

The rapid growth in E/BD teacher education programs began in 1963 with the passage of Public Law 88-164, The Mental Retardation Facilities and Community Mental Health Centers Construction Act of 1963. This law provided money to support teacher preparation programs and student stipends. Federal dollars supported 20 new programs in 1968, as well as 50 established programs of the 132 operating in various concentrations at that time (Tompkins, 1969).

In 1992–1993 (U.S. Department of Education, 1995), the schools employed about 30,000 teachers of students with E/BD and reported a need for 4,600 more. About 0.71% of the school-age population was served as having E/BD, far less than the 2% federal estimate for serious emotional disturbance and the 10% most mental health professionals cite.

Today, we have complex programs to prepare teachers of children with E/BD. Some programs operate full time by using student stipends, while others train part-time students who are teaching full time in general education settings. Most programs do both. Programs have progressed from a list of courses to a list of outcomes that students must know and be able to do as teachers. While that is indeed good progress, we do not know what happens to children if all of those outcomes are applied effectively. If they are as effective as we professionals think they are, maybe the children will do as well as the graduates of my mother's prairie school. We can but hope!

People and Events

2

Any person who attempts to describe people or events that have influenced the field of special education for children with E/BD runs the risk of leaving important people and/or events out of the narrative. I am willing to take that risk, with the caveat that my response is personal, one that is based upon the events and people who have had a significant impact upon my professional career, especially the earlier days of excitement associated with new program development.

Influential People in E/BD

The first significant books that I encountered when I entered the field were written by Fritz Redl and David Wineman, *Children Who Hate* and *Controls from Within*. These two books were later combined into one volume, *The Aggressive Child* (1957). Redl and Wineman developed their strategies for understanding behavior and therapeutic interventions through direct observations of children who were disturbed and were disturbing to other people. Their work has stood the test of time and has been further elaborated by colleagues such as William Morse (1965), who developed the crisis teacher concept and many of the applications associated with Redl's and Wineman's interventions. Nicholas Long and colleagues (Fagen, Long, & Stevens, 1975) elaborated on the psychoeducational model and further developed programs that enable children with E/BD to acquire self-control. Finally, the book *Conflict in the Classroom* (Long, Morse, & Newman, 1996) has withstood the test of time dating from its first publication in 1965. This book is a goldmine of ways to better understand the children we serve, as well as providing specific intervention procedures based on a psychoeducational model.

Much of the leadership for development of teacher education programs can also be traced to a timely study by William Morse, Richard Cutler, and Albert Fink (1964) dealing with the status of public school classes for the emotionally handicapped—children whom we now identify as having E/BD—in the early 1960s. Anybody involved in developing and implementing a teacher education program surely used their book as a valuable resource for components to include in a professional preparation curriculum. Seven types of programs were identified, ranging from absolute chaos to psychodynamic to applied behavior analysis and finally to horribly punitive.

The two professionals most associated with the development of a structured model of teacher preparation were Norris Haring (Haring & Phillips, 1962) and Frank Hewett (1968). Haring is the person who talked me out of leaving a good position as director of education at the Children's Hospital of the Menninger Clinic to join him in setting up a research and demonstration classroom in the Children's Rehabilitation Unit at the University of Kansas Medical Center. We had concurrently identified a set of procedures that seemed to be effective in educating children with E/BD. Basically, that system or concept was one of *structure*, defined as the clarification of the relationships among behaviors and the events that precede and follow them. At the same time that Haring and I were involved in that work, Hewett was conducting similar research on the engineered classroom in the California public schools.

Once a person goes beyond the specific language associated with models of teaching children with E/BD (as well as preparing teachers for them), it is clear that supporters of various models are advocating similar kinds of knowledge and skills. Who would deny the importance of interpersonal relationships in working with these children? Who would deny the importance of competence as a teacher in working with these children? And who would deny the importance of conducting evaluations of whether what we do as teachers makes any difference in the lives of these children? For example, the measurement principles associated with a structured model can be applied effectively to the life-space interventions (Naslund, 1987) that Long (1974) has so clearly explicated for children with E/BD. The measurement process associated with the structured or applied behavior analysis approach is neutral, and, as I have demonstrated in other studies (Whelan, 1998), can be applied across the board whether one adopts the philosophies associated with psychoeducational, intrapsychic, or behavioral models of understanding behavior. In my view, a very significant event has been the melding of different theoretical models of understanding behaviors (more about this later) that society labels as deviant and the interventions that can be applied to bring them back into a circle of what society determines to constitute normalcy.

I do not mean to imply that models of teaching cannot be used injudiciously. They can, and there are examples of that happening. A person who attempts a life-space intervention without adequate preparation and supervision is stepping into deep waters indeed. Similarly, a person who equates punishment with structure is making a monumental error that does an injustice not only to the children upon whom it is perpetrated, but also upon the profession itself. In brief, the various models of understanding children and helping them develop more functional lives are neutral. People learn how to apply them and in some instances misapply them. The latter should be rooted out of our profession.

A major contribution to our field was the Conceptual Project directed by William Rhodes (1972). It took a great effort to catalogue major theories, associated interventions, and applied practices. It is still valid today and, I hope, required reading for all doctoral students in E/BD.

As I indicated at the beginning of this chapter, I am sure that I have left out people who deserved to be recognized. There have been many colleagues involved in our little piece of special education for many years. These colleagues are the students of the very people that I listed. So, in that respect, when I listed those individuals, I also included all of their students, and all of the students of their students, and the students to come in future years.

Significant Events in E/BD

In terms of events, one only has to look at Michael Bower's (1969) research in California on the early identification of children with emotional disabilities, the study by Morse and colleagues on the status of classrooms for these youngsters in 1964, and, more recently, the follow-up study done by Jane Knitzer and colleagues titled *At the Schoolhouse Door* (Knitzer, Steinberg, & Fleisch, 1990). When one compares the Morse and Knitzer studies, some interesting trends can be discerned, and not all of them are in a positive direction. For example, in 1964 curriculum was observed to be remedial in its emphasis, whereas in 1990 it was defined largely by worksheets and seatwork. In 1964, management of children's inappropriate behaviors included life-space interventions, learning self-control, high expectations for performance, and positive consequences for meeting academic and social goals. In 1990, by contrast, behavior management seemed to focus on classroom silence instead of student learning. One positive note in 1990 was the observation that school-based mental health services appeared to be increasing.

A project that created great interest, but few policy changes, was the substantial work of Nicholas Hobbs (1975) centering on deviant behaviors and their classification. The proposed model for classifying children is similar to what is now called an *individualized education program (IEP)*.

In summarizing my thoughts on this topic, I want to emphasize the importance of understandings and interventions that withstand the test of time. They are the field's memory banks. While, for example, we do not see many references at this point to the engineered classroom developed by Hewett, the concepts of that model are being followed in many classrooms and teacher education programs throughout the country. Also, although we do not hear much about the structured model developed by Haring, again the concepts are followed extensively in many classrooms. At the same time, there are teachers who are following Morse's crisis teacher model and using all of the psychoeducational knowledge and skills at their command to ensure programming excellence for children with E/BD. It is sad to note that at times many teachers are practicing good professional strategies but probably have little inkling of the tremendous toil and cost that went into developing them by leaders in our field. Both past and present events must be learned and honored because, in spite of what we might preach from time to time, we do not make decisions for the future; we can only contemplate how our current decisions will play out in the future. I am hopeful that teacher education programs will continue to meld and develop even more strongly effective strategies associated with different models of behavioral understandings and interventions, be they intrapsychic, psychoeducational, behavioral, cognitive restructuring, self-empowerment, or whatever new label comes along to describe old, but valuable, contributions to the field.

In addition to the people and events I have cited, there are other important events that should be recognized. One that comes to mind immediately is a pivotal study by Lee Robins titled *Deviant Children Grown Up* (1966). From this study, we learned the importance of preparing teachers to deal with chronic aggression by children with E/BD and how difficult it is to change behaviors once they have been learned and practiced. This difficulty shows up in the long-term pattern of deviance even after children leave special education programs that enabled them to use strategies for controlling their behaviors while they were enrolled. The fact that a program did not inoculate them against future kinds of problems speaks more to the issue of support and maintenance of these children as they grew older than it does to the effectiveness of the prior intervention program. Another pivotal study is reflected in the work of Herbert Quay (Quay & Werry, 1986) and the methods developed to categorize certain patterns of deviancy. These methods are important because they are functional for use in teacher preparation, as well as for understanding children who may find their way into special classrooms for students with E/BD. Unlike psychiatric nosology, the functional approach used clusters of observable behavior to classify a problem as, for instance, *socialized aggressive.*

There are many studies in the literature that demonstrate that applied behavior analysis works with children with E/BD. There are also studies that demonstrate that modification of curriculum can have a more profound impact on such measures as attention to task, reduction of deviant behaviors, and increased academic scores than all of the M&Ms ever used as reinforcers. There are studies that show that effective life-space intervention provides insight that can be used by children to modify their behavior. In other words, the studies in our literature have demonstrated that when we work with the continuum of events that occur before behavior, the behavior itself, and events after the behavior, much can be accomplished in enabling children to experience success in school, at home, and in the community.

A Peek Through the Kaleidoscope

I cannot resist the opportunity to elaborate once more about our theoretical foundations. Figure 2.1 is a simplified display of the three major theoretical approaches to understanding the behavior of students with E/BD. The theories are generally well known, but for the purposes of illustration, I will briefly identify them here.

Intrapsychic Model

The longest-standing theory is known as the *intrapsychic* approach to understanding the origin or development of emotional problems. While Figure 2.1 does not do justice to the complexities of this approach to understanding behavior, its boxes emphasize the major tenets of the basic theory. Prior events of a traumatic or chaotic nature are believed to produce anxiety in the person who experiences those events. Because anxiety is an aversive situation, one that individuals tend to want to avoid or to escape from at any opportunity, its presence tends to be repressed—that is, put out of awareness by any number of means including behaviors that are said to be symptomatic of an underlying cause. Unfortunately, the act of avoiding and escaping or getting rid of even an awareness that one has anxieties never puts the anxieties totally out of mind, even though one cannot bring them to an awareness level at will. The repression makes itself known in terms of a person's distortion of what most people might perceive as reality. For example, let's assume that a student's first encounter with a teacher is chaotic and aversive. Because the events are so painful, it produces anxiety to the extent that the student does not want to experience that situation again. In attempting to get rid of the anxiety, the student represses the experience or puts it out of conscious awareness because of its painful memories. However, in future encounters with another teacher, the student may behave in ways that reflect how he or she had coped with the same situation that precipitated the original or prior events. This, in turn, leads to observed behavior that people might label as symptomatic or characteristic of a child with emotional disorders.

The intervention tasks using the intrapsychic approach are designed to enable the individual to relive (e.g., role play, verbalizations) the prior events in a nonjudgmental, nonevaluative environment. The rationale behind this is that if a person can bring these past experiences out into the open, examine them realistically with the support of others, and understand that they are influencing current behavior, the new insight or understanding may lead to behavior changes. The supportive individual who helps another reach this understanding is also suggesting ways or methods of coping with the reality of the day-to-day world. This combination of self-understanding and attempts to respond in more efficient and effective ways can lead to improvement of the problems originally observed. The person with understanding and insight can say, "Yes, that original teacher was indeed very punishing, but that is not my problem, and I must approach each new teacher with a relatively open mind and make determinations based upon the current interactions between us and not events from the past." Of course, no child talks like this, but the idea is clear.

In practice, there are probably many teachers who use this approach on a daily basis, although they may not be aware that they

Figure 2.1 Relationship between and among a behavior and various models that explain its occurrence

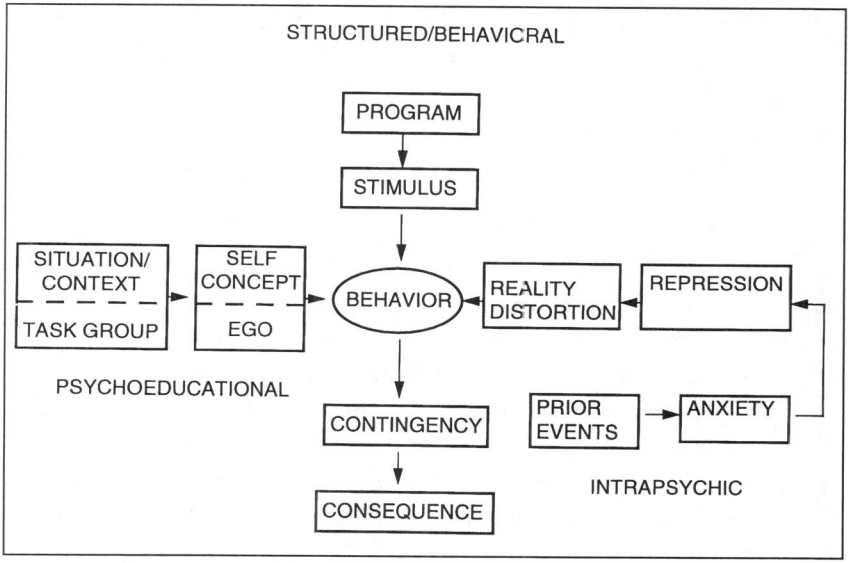

are using part of the intrapsychic theory and its related intervention procedures. They do not run individual therapy groups or counseling sessions. But each day, and with a variety of students, they may have the opportunity to make clear statements such as, "You are treating me as if I've done something very bad to you. I haven't done anything bad to you, so let's talk about this and see if we can solve the problems." The teacher at that point is attempting to help a student achieve insight into behavior that is not realistic in terms of existing conditions.

Psychoeducational Model

This model or theory places emphasis on the development of the ego within the individual and mostly plays down Freudian concepts of the id and superego. As can be seen in Figure 2.1, behavior is observed and analyzed in terms of the situation or context in which it occurs. Specifically, what is the group situation and what is the task to be performed by the group or by individuals within the group? This situational context is then filtered through the student's self-concept or ego. For example, students with very negative or poor self-concepts tend to act out those conditions even though situations or contexts do not call for it. In addition, the so-called *ego that does not perform* is characterized by behaviors that are described as deviant or noncompliant. That is, a student's ego state has not developed to the point where it can separate out the realities of a situation and respond accordingly.

A prime example of intervention using a psychoeducational model is the life-space interview. A brief explanation of this process, which, of course, does not do justice to the complexity of the adult–student encounter, includes three basic and essential questions that are asked in a crisis situation. For instance, assume that a student has had a major blow-up in class and has thrown a book on the floor. The teacher and student go to a place removed from the group to discuss the incident. It may be called a *safe place*. Once the student has calmed down to the point where communication can be initiated, the teacher may ask the student to give her perception of what happened. During the student's explanation of the "blow-up," the teacher may be sensitive to opportunities to comment in a nonevaluative manner and point out alternative ways of looking at the situation that precipitated the disintegration of self-control. For instance, the teacher might ask, "Did Billy's comment really cause the upset, or were you really stressed about something else?" A second question would be to ask the student how she feels about the event. This is likely to elicit a verbal response of anger, disappointment, and hurt. These expressions are far more desirable than physical expressions of the loss of self-control via breaking furniture, throwing books, or hitting other people. The teachable moment comes with the third question, "What happens the next time something like this occurs?" It is through this process that the teacher and student attempt to problem solve and develop strategies for the future. For example, if the event was precipitated by another student making an obscene gesture, then the teacher and student may think of ways to ignore the gesture if it happens in the future or to behave in ways that do not result in a loss of self-control.

The advantage of the psychoeducational model is that it deals with the here and now. A teacher can use current encounters to plan more effective strategies in dealing with day-to-day activities in the future. The model includes many different ways of managing behaviors, as well as helping students achieve insight and understanding of what elicits their behavior in any given situation.

Structured/Behavioral Model

This model has observable events occurring after the behavior, whereas the other two include only prior, or antecedent, events. The structured/behavioral model has two antecedent events and two events that occur after the behavior has been elicited. The antecedent part of this model includes what is known as a *program*. For educators, the program, or schedule, can be identified as a part of or prerequisite to a specific assignment. It is the sequence through which, as Figure 2.1 indicates, the stimulus (i.e., task assignment) is presented to a student. The task may be a single word in a reading lesson or a single arithmetic problem during a computation lesson or a variety of other tasks that the student might be expected to complete. These tasks do not necessarily need to be just for individuals; they can be associated with a group project or event or a playground activity. The program usually is the frequency of presenting tasks (e.g., 1 per minute, 20 per lesson). It sets a structure that enables a student to know when and what type of task expectation will be presented in a teaching and learning environment. The presentation of the task (stimulus) according to a set schedule elicits a behavior.

While it is true that various antecedent events can elicit behaviors that most educators would consider desirable, it is also true that these prior events can elicit behaviors that are undesirable (e.g., gang behavior or behavior that draws negative attention from educators). The educator's important responsibility is to select developmentally appropriate tasks and to schedule their presentation in a manner that elicits prosocial behaviors from students. Let's label the two antecedents something really outlandish: *curriculum*.

The parts of the model that follow the behavior are the contingency and the *consequence*. The consequence is an event that follows the behavior. This event can be positive in the sense that it will increase the probability that the behavior will occur again. For example, if a student does all his math problems correctly and gets an A+, as well as a word of encouragement from the teacher, and if, indeed, this consequence has meaning and satisfaction for the student, then it is likely that the behavior will increase in frequency or will at least be maintained. The *contingency* part of the sequence involves the frequency or ratio with which the consequence is provided after the behavior has occurred. For instance, not every 100% paper may be followed by a specific consequence. Instead, the requirement may be to have several themes for the consequence; the contingency could be three well-written themes before the consequence is delivered. Therefore, the contingency would be a ratio of three responses (i.e., themes) to one consequence (i.e., the opportunity to be teacher's assistant).

There are several points of intervention using a structured/behavioral model. A teacher can manage the stimulus dimension and the program through which it is presented to the student in order to elicit a response. An example of this would be modification of the material itself. Because so much of the deviant behavior that educators observe is due to students' attempts to escape and avoid failure situations, presentation of curriculum that can enhance the probability of successful responding can reduce deviant behaviors while simultaneously enhancing the acquisition of prosocial behaviors. The other part of the model that a teacher can use to enable a student to develop self-control and more effective cognitive ways of problem solving uses the contingency and consequence dimension. For example, it is not unknown for students described as predelinquent or delinquent to work very hard on prosocial types of activities for the opportunity to ride in a limousine or to earn tokens that can be cashed in for other events (e.g., a pizza party, the opportunity to go to a movie or rent a videotape).

The preceding discussion is full of intellectual, heuristic, "stuff." However if we discount the description of an intellectual as "a person who is educated far beyond a recorded IQ," we are still left with the question: Does the student care about all of this theory prattle? Probably not, but teachers need to care.

Common Ground for Understanding

The three hot-air balloons in Figure 2.2 illustrate the major theoretical models of understanding the behavior of students with E/BD. Notice the proponents of each theory in the baskets. Our theorists are observing the *same* child–teacher interaction in a classroom. How do they explain the interaction? It might be expressed as follows:

- Intrapsychic Model

  The child's demand to work on the model plane is in the service of primary gain, a way to decrease anxiety generated by past shame of incompetent performance.

- Psychoeducational Model

  The child's temptation resistance is low because the ego is not strong enough to delay gratification.

- Structured/Behavioral Model

  The child is showing part of a behavior chain associated with complex avoidance and escape behaviors.

In Figure 2.2, the teacher is using structure to substantiate positive, approach behaviors to what the student has in the past experienced as aversive interactions. If the task is within the student's performance capability, then the plane building (high-probability behavior) just may motivate a few math solutions (low-probability behavior). If the teacher can ensure multiple successes with math, the student will learn to approach it as well as model building.

How does the teacher respond when using the other two models? A teacher from the intrapsychic model might respond thus: "He has a great deal of anxiety now, so I am going to support his efforts to deal

Figure 2.2   *Applying models to real situations in classrooms*

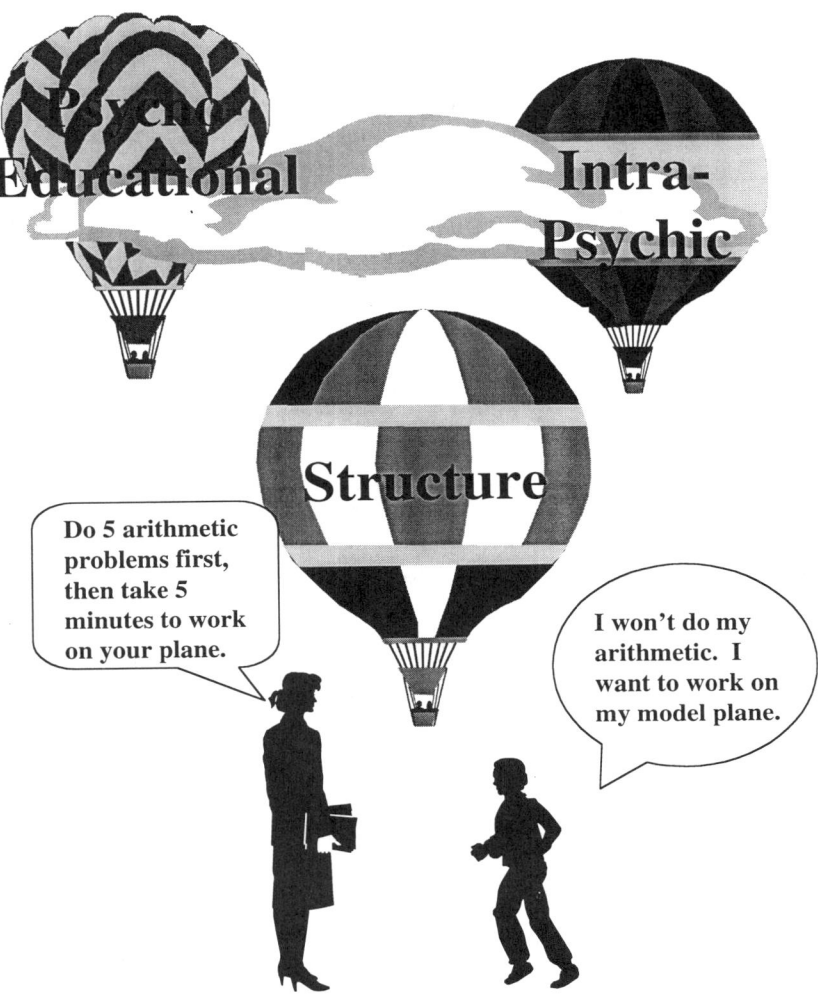

with it through our relationship. With time and therapy, he will use our relationship to acquire a love for learning." A teacher using a psychoeducational model might respond this way: "I should have removed the airplane from view. Now he is focused on it exclusively. I don't want to force him into a tantrum by insisting that he do this task now, so I will help him over this block by substituting a different type of expectation."

Which one of the three models works? The answer is that they all do, with some students, in some situations, and at some times. Conceptually, the key is to know the models as foundations and the applications associated with them, then look at the student's reactions to determine whether they work. One way to reduce the three balloons to one with all of the theorists in one basket is to learn the language of each model. It is too much to hope for a common language in our field; trying to understand each other is the next best thing if we truly care about helping students with E/BD improve their performance at home, in the community, and at school.

You don't believe there is a common ground for understanding? What if I told you that Freud and Skinner were "two peas from the same theoretical pod?" Freud believed that the sources of energy used to produce behaviors were many instincts, mostly without names. Instincts produce psychic energy that is used to drive a variety of behaviors. Now then, what is this *instinct* described by Freud, and how does Skinner, the great behaviorist, fit into the mold? Table 2.1 provides the answer. The intrapsychic column lists Freud's four basic parts or features of an instinct. Under the behavioral column are the terms that Skinner used to identify the same phenomena or observations identified by Freud. Finally, the middle column displays the common language we all use for understanding behavior.

Close inspection of the table indicates that Freud had two features for what Skinner called a stimulus. Both Freud and Skinner recognized that something is necessary to evoke behavior. Both believed that behavior had a goal-seeking function, tension reduction for Freud (Aim), and a pleasurable outcome for Skinner in the form of positive reinforcement or a consequence. In fact, the only thing Freud missed was Skinner's unique use of a contingency that controlled how the consequence was delivered (e.g., for every response or on some type of variable schedule). Both giants in our field obviously were entranced with how people learn, and through their observations—scientific or not—developed their models of explain-

Table 2.1
Features of an Instinct

Intrapsychic (Freud)	Common Language	Behavioral (Skinner)
Source	Need/push	Stimulus
Impetus	Need strength	
Object	Behavior that is goal directed	Response
Aim	Reduce need as goal	Consequence

ing behavior. Interventions, still used today, were spun off these models.

Still not convinced? An intrapsychic concept of why a symptom is difficult to eliminate is that it reduces anxiety, an aversive situation in any model. Reducing anxiety is called *primary gain* in the intrapsychic model, but in the structured model, it is called *negative reinforcement*. Any behavior that reduces anxiety or an aversive situation is likely to increase or be stable in frequency; hence the rationale for the development of symptoms. Symptoms also have secondary gain. After all, if you are sick, people take care of you. Skinner called this *positive reinforcement*. A behavior that produces pleasurable consequences is likely to be maintained or to increase in frequency.

A Look at the Dark Side

Writing about this subtopic is extremely difficult simply because I cannot think of a reasonably common-sense professional practice that has failed to produce results. Instead, the failure has been in the misuse of the practice. That is, people who try to apply it are not trained well, or personnel preparation programs have not incorporated the practice within their curriculum and have not ensured that students can demonstrate the practice prior to termination of their formal training.

Of course, one can point to terrible misapplications of practices. One example is using contingent electrical shock even when it is purported to be done under scientific conditions; another is the willingness to jump on bandwagons of "one size fits all" interventions, such as listing rules on the chalkboard and then applying the same consequence to all children, whether they work or not. Another failed practice is the complete misinterpretation of Skinner's principles of operant conditioning through overuse of the punishment procedure and underuse of reinforcement for increasing prosocial and appropriate performance in school and home settings—currently described as "positive behavioral interventions" in federal law.

Another failed practice has been the almost universal misunderstanding of what special education is or is not. As a field—and this is just not associated with E/BD programs—we have tended to concentrate on categories to the exclusion of what special education really is. Special education is described in federal law as specially designed instruction to meet the unique needs of a child with a disability, in this case a child with E/BD. If anything, our service and personnel preparation programs probably have not devoted enough attention to the "specially designed instruction" clause of the definition. For example, in conducting a preinstructional assessment, how many trials do we insist that a teacher candidate complete before we are reasonably confident that the knowledge and skills have been mastered? We know from clinical evidence that most of us may need 25 or 35 trials before even the first step of mastery is accomplished. This approach to learning requires a great deal of time, but given the cost of not doing it, reflected in the lives of children with E/BD, I do not believe we can afford to do less. Running through a preinstructional assessment just one time should in no way be reported as the attainment of mastery.

Yet another failed policy is the lack of a nationwide approach to prevention and gaps in interagency services for children with E/BD. We read such words as "seamless," "wraparound," and "integrated" to describe interagency services that children with E/BD and their families need. The agencies include education, mental health, and social welfare. The failure to develop a coordinated system of services is matched only by our unwillingness to place resources at the prevention end of the continuum. These failures are not of recent origin, as attested to by the prevention- and intervention-oriented community mental health programs that were conceptualized in the early 1960s. The resources to implement some very well designed plans were not forthcoming at federal, state, and local levels. Of course, there are exceptions, and there are some well-run community mental health centers, but upon careful examination, it is difficult to see how their services are integrated with the needs of the children and their families.

Some Promising Practices

3

Probably the most important promising practice that I have observed within the past 5 years is the wholesale adoption by general education of special education principles. Examples include an individualized instruction approach, authentic assessment, outcomes-oriented programs of service and training, interdisciplinary programming, students who keep their records of progress, and student-led parent–teacher conferences. If successful special education practices continue to be incorporated into general education classrooms, maybe the prevention aspect of reducing the numbers of children with E/BD can truly take hold in the near future.

As described previously, I believe that a good emerging practice is the continued development and widespread dissemination of successful strategies of behavioral understanding and interventions associated with the psychoeducational and the structured/behavioral models. For example, the increased emphasis on enabling children to acquire self-control skills could produce decreases in violent acts associated with impulsive thoughts. Many more examples could be listed. Furthermore, I believe there should be a renewed emphasis upon returning to the principle that children are the very best teachers. Even though we, as professional teacher educators, have preached for many years that we should observe children's responses to the environment, we often neglect that admonition in our day-to-day practices. How often, for example, have all of us read in the literature that an item was used as a reinforcer but that the behavior didn't change? This is not only completely contradictory to the principles that Skinner (1953) advocated, but also an impossibility. An event cannot be a reinforcer unless it is demonstrated to function that way.

Current
Issues

4

Decertification

A very serious issue is the move to decertify children as having E/BD and to exclude them from the school system. There are high dollar costs associated with serving children with E/BD and preparing specialists who will help them overcome their problems. Excluding children from school, however, is not a solution. If anything, this strategy will only increase costs in the future. That consequence has been demonstrated many times by increases in the prison population and dependence upon a welfare system that is also costly.

Let's see how decertification might work on a group of students identified as having E/BD and another group of general education students. First, we ask respondents to complete a checklist (Kelly, 1990) that sorts students into three groups, those with (a) emotional, (b) conduct, or (c) no disorders. What happens to our sample of students with E/BD? The results are that 67% of them are in the emotional disorders category and 33% fall under the conduct disorders category. Therefore, as a special educational administrator, I can decertify 33 out of every 100 E/BD students served because under federal regulations students with conduct disorders (socially maladjusted) are not eligible for special education and related services. Now I can cut my budget by one third, thereby making the superintendent and the schoolboard happy. But wait, it gets even better. My 67 students in the emotional disorders category also have a conduct score. So, if I select the students who have a higher conduct than emotional score, the emotional disorders group drops to 15, a 75% budget reduction. Surely, the superintendent will give me a large bonus for saving so much money; the football team will prosper. Is this scenario farfetched? Probably. However, it is not an impossible event. I am hopeful that vigilance will keep it from coming to pass.

Growth of Alternative Schools

Along with decertification is the increased growth of alternative schools. As a school administrator, I see dollar savings in removing children who are troubled and troublesome from the general education environment and placing them in an alternative school. If they cannot function there, they can be removed from the educational system and turned over to some other agency of government as clients to be served. This strategy produces big dollar savings for school boards and reduces conflicts for administrators, but it is also flawed public policy. A dollar saved now will be spent tenfold in the future. However, if the alternative schools were based upon a Re-ED model (Hobbs, 1964), which they are not, I would support that part of the service continuum without reservation.

Recruitment and Employment Issues

There are increasing shortages of adequately prepared personnel to serve children with E/BD (American Association for Employment in Education, 1998). As many teacher educators know, it is getting more and more difficult to recruit teachers into this field because of the stresses associated with it and also because of the onerous paperwork that teachers must complete to comply with federal and state laws. Every hour devoted to forms of questionable validity reduces the potential for effective use of instructional time. Resources are too few to employ support personnel to deal with the paperwork.

Another current issue is the tendency to use personnel other than teachers to spend all day with a child who has a serious E/BD problem. It could be that the paraeducator is very good and has a strong relationship with the youngster, but are the interactions that should enhance growth and development planned and completed?

Personnel Preparation Programs

Finally, I don't know whether our personnel preparation programs are doing enough to prepare graduates to respond effectively to the violence they will encounter in the schools, not only among the general population, but also among children labeled as having E/BD. For example, the U.S. General Accounting Office (1995) has cited statistics showing that (a) about 3,000,000 crimes occur in or near schools each year, about 1 every 6 seconds during school hours; (b) 105 school-related violent deaths occurred between 1992 and 1994; and (c) parents view school order and safety as a top priority for action. Similar increases were noted at the elementary school level. To claim that these increases in violence are not associated with students in special education, would be erroneous. A survey in Kansas (Cooley, 1995) showed that only 6 in 1,000 students in general education were suspended for violations, whereas 14 in 1,000 students in special education were suspended. Unsurprisingly, at least to people associated with the field of E/BD, about 44% of all the special education suspensions were for children with E/BD. The surprising fact was that roughly the same percentage was accorded to students with learning disabilities (LD). It makes one wonder about the difference between the two populations served. However, students with LD make up 5% of the general school population, while students with E/BD represent only 1%. The two groups together represent 11% of all students, general and special, suspended or expelled.

By far the most important issue that needs to be addressed now and in the future is teacher education for personnel who serve children with E/BD. I am not going to launch into a history of personnel preparation strategies; Robert Zabel (1988) has done that very well.

In addition, Richard Simpson, Robert Zabel, and I completed an article on special education personnel preparation (Simpson, Whelan, & Zabel, 1993), and I also completed a chapter about developing standards for special education teacher certification (Whelan, 1991). These citations provide a detailed review of the elements that constitute a teacher preparation program.

I want to use this space to provide a brief narrative of what the field might think about for the near future, long after I have retired to the golf course. If I were to develop a teacher education program to prepare teachers of children with E/BD, I would start anew and undertake the following efforts. First, I would line up professors from the School of Social Welfare who have professional preparation and experience in schools as social workers. Second, I would line up the very best teacher educators in developmental, corrective, and remedial instruction. Third, I would line up experts who know intrapsychic, psychoeducational, structured, and applied behavior analysis models. Finally, I would insist that all faculty members have a strong commitment to program evaluation, not only as it exists within the teacher preparation program, but also as applied to what graduates accomplish as they interact with children in educational settings. These three groups exist today, and there are no real barriers that preclude organizing them into a strong teacher education cluster of inquiry and practice.

This strong group of teacher educators would prepare teachers who can be effective in understanding, prevention, and intervention. It might take 2 years to do so, but it would be worth the time and effort. The teacher education program would focus on providing didactic experiences in classrooms and integrate field experiences that exemplify the best practices in the field. Program graduates would be equally able to function within instructional contexts as teachers, consultants to teachers in general education, and clinicians in home and community settings. These professionals would be prepared to function as case managers who bring personnel together from other agencies to provide services to children and their family members.

The rationale for including the family and agency work is that school uses only one fourth of a 24-hour day. The rest of the day is devoted to activities in the home and in the community. So this particular model would prepare professionals who understand that children, if they are to have a full chance in life, must have the services of the school and every other social agency that may influence or guide them.

Based upon insights and understandings obtained from a child's performance at school, in the home, and in the community, this professional could use a variety of interventions. Individual counseling with the child might be a strategy, or intensive individualized instruction of a corrective or remedial nature might be employed. Visitations in which the professional observed the interaction of a child with E/BD in a family setting might give clues for interventions that could be implemented in the home itself. The important aspect of this approach is that this person could be available to step in immediately in a prevention capacity, or if intervention was needed, whenever a child showed signs of not progressing as expected.

But what do we call this "super professional"? How about *teacher* as a novel idea!

Parting
Comments

5

I am glad that James Kauffman is writing the *Futures* part of this monograph. My historical part is by far the easier of the tasks, although others might have selected different historical markers from the ones I have emphasized here. Kauffman's job of looking into the future is riskier, because 20 years from now there will undoubtedly be some old curmudgeon around to let him know how accurate his predictions were.

The following parting comments are not my own. I am ending as I started, with some "oldies but goodies"—knowledge that is forever new in its use if not in its origins.

The first comment is a quote to guide us in planning educational experiences for students with special needs. Read it carefully, and use it every day:

> To leave a child wholly to his own inclinations in learning is as absurd as to send him to take honey from a swarm of angry bees and not expect him to be stung. To supply him with honey, all that he wants, at all times and without exertion to himself, is to clog his taste and destroy his appetite. We must see that he is led to look for the sweet, taught to recognize it when he finds it, and to extract it from the comb. He will enjoy working to get it. On the other hand, he must not be sent where the reward is too difficult to find and secure, lest he become discouraged and cease to work. (Sylvester, 1909, p. 99)

Finally, I want to urge our colleagues in other areas of special education who want to include all in general education programs to read what one of our pioneers had to say about this laudable philosophy:

> According to general assumptions, it is expected that disturbed children should improve if they are exposed to a good educational setting and surrounded by friendly people who handle them with wisdom and affection. . . .
>
> Moreover, we take it for granted that the sight of the happy and desirable behavior displayed by companions who are less disturbed than they should make bad children eager to mend their ways, especially if they find out that they can gain love and approval of friendly and generous adults by doing so. Besides, we assume that the mere absence of the cruelty, abuse, insult, and embarrassment which these children have experienced before should give them a chance to blossom out into feelings of warmth, acceptedness, and happy security. . . .
>
> From our description of the egos of the children who hate and of some of their superego diseases it is clear that these children are not ready to benefit from a "good educational set-up" at all. They meet none of the prerequisites which even so "simple" a thing as a "good educational diet" presupposes as a condition for having effect. . . .
>
> In short, good education is *not* enough for the cure of the children who hate. Rather, the reverse comes closer to the truth: in order for a good educational diet to take hold of these children at all, their basic ego disturbances must be repaired first. (Redl & Wineman, 1957, p. 240)

Students with E/BD are placed in specially designed programs that get them ready to be included in and prosper from general education experiences. Our job, past, present, and future, is to help them get ready. That is a big challenge, one that should keep our teaching, research, and service initiatives at a very high level of activity.

Redl and Wineman (1957) also said that weekly psychotherapy sessions do not work any better than general education. In fact, the sessions probably do not work as well. Our students with E/BD need something before general education and therapy will produce results, and that something is us, caring professional special educators who know "what, when, where, and how" to do with students and their families. Our past was turbulent but exciting in what we learned. It is a sure bet that our future will bring even more excitement, learning, and well-deserved successes.

PART II

FUTURE DIRECTIONS

James M. Kauffman

Introduction

In his monograph contribution to the CCBD conference, Richard J. Whelan has shared a wonderful historical perspective on our work. The knowledge and wisdom he has gained by working with other great leaders in our field from about mid-century to the present illustrate why he is a national treasure and why so many of us are proud to claim him as a friend and mentor. Like so many others around the country, I am more deeply indebted to him than to anyone else for my professional development. But in no way should my mistakes and failings be attributed to him. As Mark Twain said, "You can straighten a worm, but the crook is in him and only waiting." If I fail, it is not because Dick Whelan didn't try to straighten me up.

Whelan's historical account of the field set the stage for me to try to peer over the horizon and guess what is coming. While I think many others are better qualified than I to talk about the future, I agreed to offer my thoughts. My comments will, without doubt, be ridiculed by some, perhaps sooner rather than later, and probably for good reasons. I hope I have the long life and the grace to laugh at myself 20 years hence, to see the humor in how off target my comments were. My accuracy rate will likely be worse than the typical person achieves in a game of Pin the Tail on the Donkey. Knowing this, I'm going to avoid some potential mistakes by not making predictions. Instead, I'm going to discuss what I hope will happen and what I think we need to try to avoid.

A lot has been made of the fact that we are about to witness the change of millennia. Personally, I do not attach any particular significance to the end of a millennium or the beginning of another. Our calendar is a purely social construction. Steven Jay Gould (1997) discussed this in his book *Questioning the Millennium. A Rationalist's Guide to a Precisely Arbitrary Countdown.* I recommend it as a thoughtful and entertaining little book with a surprise at the end having to do with disability. Regardless of our calendar, though, we are at what seems to me a peculiar point in our professional evolution. It is a point at which special education is being attacked by many people—including some special educators—not all of whom are interested in our professional survival. And we are being pulled in many different directions, not all of which lead to happier days for children with emotional and behavioral disorders.

Since what lies over the horizon is anybody's guess, I will concentrate here on what I hope we will see and what I think we need to guard against if my hopes are to become realities. I'm going to focus on just four things that I think are most important to a happier future:

1. Recognition that antisocial behavior is disabling and requires special education intervention.

2. Widespread implementation of effective prevention procedures.

3. Making our priority in multicultural education finding and embracing the common or universal.

4. Commitment to finding and using scientific or common knowledge as the basis for promoting best practices.

Recognizing That Antisocial Behavior Is Disabling

My first hope is that we will recognize that antisocial behavior is disabling and requires special education intervention. For the past quarter century, we have been stuck with a federal definition that fosters a disinclination to serve children and youth who exhibit behavior that can be considered maladjusted or a conduct disorder. Many school authorities—including some in special education—use the social maladjustment exclusion in the federal definition to avoid taking any responsibility for youngsters with one of the most serious, devastating disorders of childhood. In my view, school administrators and legislators have been leading the way toward denial of educators' responsibility for disability of a type that angers people instead of making them sympathetic, and too many of us in special education have been inclined to follow. Neither logical arguments nor reliable empirical studies support the distinction between social maladjustment and emotional disturbance (Costenbader & Buntaine, 1999; Kauffman, 1997).

Our society does not like children with conduct disorder, and, in fact, we do not want to be tolerant of such conduct. We want better understanding of behavior and valuing of kids, but we certainly don't want people to think that conduct disorder is acceptable. We want people to recognize that conduct disorder is a *bad* thing and that we want these children changed. Tolerance for the behavior is not what we want, any more than we want acceptance of any other disease or disability as a welcome condition. What we want is recognition of the fact that we could and should avoid a lot of the deviant behavior known as conduct disorder or social maladjustment. We want the understanding that such behavior is disabling, and that special education interventions applied early and consistently to the children who begin exhibiting such conduct are among the strategies we need to practice.

I hope that just over the horizon we will see the National Mental Health and Special Education Coalition's definition accepted into federal law and regulation. It would be a great leap forward if the powerful in our society were to recognize social maladjustment or conduct disorder as a condition needing early correction by special education rather than later correction by juvenile justice. It would be progress if our society were to see the role of juvenile justice as education and rehabilitation rather than merely as containment and punishment.

What I think we need to avoid is assuming that we can somehow discriminate the emotional from the behavioral, the inner turmoil from external manifestations of it. What I hope we will stop is saying that the behavior is *not* the problem, *not* the disorder, *not* the disability. We are going to be able to take effective preventive action only if we avoid the assumption that behavior is only a manifestation of something inside, only if we start recognizing that serious misconduct in its many varieties is itself a disability.

Implementing Preventive Practices

2

The second hope I have is that we will see the widespread implementation of effective preventive practices at all levels—primary, secondary, and tertiary. We need to intervene early and effectively in schools to keep behavioral disorders from developing at all if we can or to catch problems in their earliest stages and reverse their trajectory so that they do not get worse. For children who are already exhibiting behavioral disorders, I hope we will learn more about how to step in early in the chain of events so that they have fewer serious episodes of misconduct. I expanded on this idea in an article recently published in *Exceptional Children* (Kauffman, in press a).

Everybody I have ever talked to says, "Oh, yes, we should practice prevention," and the reasons they give are obvious: Prevention would save a lot of money, not to mention human misery. And yet, although everybody seems to be in agreement that we should do prevention, we do not do it consistently in our schools. In fact, what I have come to understand is that we are not going to do much prevention unless we change our thinking significantly. Our actions say that we believe that, in the end, other things are more important.

I want to list and comment briefly on what I see as some of the forces running counter to prevention. Remember that prevention means early identification and early, effective intervention. But we raise objections that have some legitimacy, and in the end we decide that these concerns override our desire for prevention. Therefore, we fail to take preventive action. Here are a dozen ways we do it—that is, a dozen ways we prevent prevention:

1. We express overriding concern for labels and stigma. Now, you can treat everybody the same without labels, but you cannot address individual needs without labels. So, for any child who needs something atypical, no label means no special services and no prevention.

2. We object to a medical model and failure-driven services. But prevention is, by definition, focusing on the avoidance of failure. If we do not anticipate a failure, we will not do prevention.

3. We prefer false negatives to false positives. We would rather risk the disaster of doing nothing about a behavioral disorder than risk doing something unnecessary, maybe because we feel we actually do more harm than good or believe that prevention is impossible.

4. We propose a paradigm shift. The upshot is that we abandon our ability to discriminate better practices from those that are not so good, so we end up saying we do not know what to do anyway.

5. We call special education ineffective, say it does not work. If you conclude that special education does not work, you will not suggest it except as a last resort under pain of legal penalty, so prevention does not have a chance.

6. We misconstrue the least restrictive environment and least intrusive intervention. We think LRE or LRI means doing the least we can, so our interventions are always too little or too late or both.

7. We protest the percentage of children receiving special services. Prevention requires identifying and serving more children. If we want to stop the growth of special education, we are not going to do prevention. We will say it's not a job for special educators; it's a job for general education.

8. We complain that special education already costs too much. Prevention may save money in the long run, but it is going to require spending more money now, and that is something most politicians and most taxpayers do not want to do now.

9. We maintain developmental optimism. We say that it is just a phase, not to worry, this one will grow out of it, no doubt. Again, we do not step in with preventive practices.

10. We denounce disproportional identification of students from ethnically and culturally diverse backgrounds. We know that minorities in America have been discriminated against and that in some cases cultural difference is misinterpreted as deviance. So in the case of a child from a diverse background, we may refuse to step in early and preventively for fear of being unfairly discriminatory or viewing ourselves as racist or being called racist.

11. We defend diversity or disability. We keep extending the range of the permissible under the guise of tolerance, and our tolerance for misbehavior keeps us from practicing prevention. After all, we're not going to prevent what we see as different but okay.

12. We deny or dodge deviance. We say that deviance is a social construct and deny the reality of the consequences for the person who exhibits deviant behavior, or we simply say that behavior is different but not deviant, unacceptable but not a disability. It is much easier to say something is not deviant or to disclaim responsibility for it than to prevent it.

I think we need to guard against letting these rationalizations keep us from practicing prevention.

Finding and Embracing the Commonalities

3

The third thing I hope for is making our priority in multicultural education finding and embracing the common or universal. I highlight this hope because I see multicultural education as one of the most important facets of our work now and in the new millennium. Currently, what I see in our approach to multiculturalism is an emphasis on diversity, on the different, the unique, the things that set cultures and people apart from each other. I am aware of the importance of understanding that people and cultures are different, but to my way of thinking there is a far more important concept that we ought to be highlighting, and that is the ways in which we are the same, the commonalities across all cultures.

It is the failure to see our common humanity that allows, if not justifies, slavery and racism and sexism. It was not any lack of recognition of difference but a lack of appreciation for sameness, for the common thread of humanity, that allowed and justified the Holocaust, apartheid, and the continuing horrors of civil wars in some of the Balkan states and some African nations. I think it is losing sight of our common humanity, our shared culture, that allows the continuation of revolting acts of violence against minorities in the United States. An emphasis on the ways people are alike, not the difference in the color of their skin or their genetic heritage, was the hallmark of Martin Luther King's civil rights movement, and that is the mark of any movement for human rights.

Today, the current is *against* finding and accentuating the common. It is acceptable and laudable in today's social environment to say that rules, expectations, curricula, management strategies, and so on do not apply to group A or group B because of their cultural difference. It is not yet seen as critical to seek and apply what is common. There is great resistance to the idea of any universal, and this rejection of the universal in favor of claiming the personal and unique is being spurred on by postmodern philosophies that reject the very idea of common knowledge or universal principles.

Two of my favorite editorial writers have commented on this notion. Ellen Goodman remarked how in marketing the assumption is that gender differences are more important than differences in interests, which may be shared across gender lines. She said, "The danger now is that the marketing moguls choose the safe route, exaggerate the differences between boys and girls, and try to mass-market by gender instead of interests" (Goodman, 1999, A8). According to Goodman, we need diversity in approaches, a diversity of options, but this diversity should not be achieved by assuming stereotypical differences based on gender or color or nation of origin.

William Raspberry wrote about how common language is getting lost in the obsession with linguistic differences. He noted, "But when we have no common shorthand—worse, when we, black and white, have two separate shorthands—it isn't just our language that gets weaker. So does some of the glue that binds us together and makes us *American*" (Raspberry, 1999, A23).

I do not want to be misunderstood. Again, *I know that we can be too quick to call our own ideas or behavior patterns or expectations universal.* We do need to recognize differences and welcome all differences that are not destructive. My point is that in our focus on diversity we are in danger of neglecting what we share and things that are, in fact, universal or nearly so. The price we will pay for this is very dear, and it will include losing the very possibility of a multicultural society that does not come apart at the seams. It is as if we have finally noticed that our cultural garment has different parts joined at the seams, and now our focus is on the seams and how each part is distinctive, not the wholeness of the garment that makes the society attractive. Pulling constantly at the seams will either result in the garment's coming apart at the seams or in its becoming misshapen and ill-fitting—something we will not want to wear. The loss of wholeness, the division into separate parts, might reduce something that could be beautiful to a pile of rags. Overemphasis on diversity and neglect of commonality—this is what we need to guard against.

Using Scientific or Common Knowledge to Promote Best Practices

4

The fourth thing I hope for is our recommitment to finding and using scientific or common knowledge as the basis for promoting best practices. I want to make clear that I do not reject all new ideas or different perspectives. But ideas are not good or helpful simply because they are new or different, nor is an idea wrong just because it is old or familiar or dominant.

Today, antiscientific sentiment is popular among many academics in the humanities and in the social sciences. *Postmodernism* and *deconstructionism* are terms often used to describe this antiscientific philosophy. I commented on this in the article I published recently in the *Journal of Special Education* (Kauffman, 1999a) and in a recent article in *Behavioral Disorders* (Kauffman, in press b), but I will reiterate briefly what I see as the essence of the problem. I think the postmodern view of things has two severe and unacceptable negative consequences for our profession. First, it offers no better solutions to problems. That is, it gives us no better tools for finding out how to improve the practice of special education or anything else. Second, and even worse, it rejects the assumption that we can actually find out that some ways of doing things are more effective than others, that there are best practices and generally ineffective practices. As I understand it, postmodernism is a call to abandon scientific understanding for the notion that there is no objective truth.

Some readers may think that I misunderstand or misinterpret, or conclude that I am needlessly, inappropriately argumentative. Maybe I am and maybe not. Let me share with you the words of someone who identifies himself as taking the postmodern view and claims he is able to explain the postmodern perspective in special education. Read carefully, and think about what it means.

> What postmodern philosophy does, among other things, is question the ability of social scientists using ANY research paradigm to "discover the truth." Basically, postmodernists hold that the idea of a neutral, disinterested researcher producing unbiased knowledge is unbelievable. . . .
>
> What postmodernists would say, and what I said in regard to [facilitated communication] FC, is that since the social scientists are unable to determine the general effectiveness of a given professional practice across cases and situations, then we should allow the served persons (students and families) the largest role possible in the decision-making process. Basically, if they want to try FC, we help them do so while making no promises about effectiveness. Try it and find out. Some find this helpful and some do not. (Source unknown)

I see this postmodern or deconstructivist position as an abdication of both science and professional responsibility. If we embrace this point of view, then we have nothing to offer the children and families we serve but hand holding. This is not the way to achieve greater social justice but a certain way of adding insult to injury. I think it is worth remembering that scientific or common knowledge and its pursuit are among the best tools we have for fighting for social justice. I imagine that the parents and children we serve are going to want functional assistance in learning, that they will ultimately condemn (and rightly, in my opinion) the academic puffery that does not provide us with better tools for solving problems. I

think parents will tell us—in fact, I think they are telling us now—
"Show us the results."

As I understand postmodernism, it is a rejection of the very idea
that we can create and use functional tools that are generally effective. It seems to be the denial of our ability to know when something
works better or does not work at all and a refusal to take professional responsibility. But postmodernism and deconstructivism are
all the rage in academic circles. The people marketing these ideas
want us to buy in to them. If we buy them, I believe we will have
bought the greatest lemon sold. And if we buy this lemon, we will
have a worthless vehicle for helping children and their families. I
readily admit—and I think most people do—that science does not
and cannot answer every important question. But to deny the
answers that science does or can give us is to embrace a philosophy
that does no good and can do great harm.

The Circle
of Courage

5

So, with these hopes and cautions in mind, what do I see as most important? Maybe the most important thing for us to do is to practice in our own professional lives the four principles Martin Brokenleg and his colleagues described as the Circle of Courage (Brendtro & Brokenleg, 1993). The Circle of Courage comes from American Indian culture, but that is not why it is helpful. It is a useful way of looking at things because it applies across cultures. It is universal, or nearly so. When the Circle of Courage is the basis for education, then we have what Brokenleg called a *reclaiming environment*—the kind of environment we want not only for the children we work with but for ourselves as well. The Circle of Courage that makes a reclaiming environment has four parts: belonging, mastery, independence, and generosity. I will comment briefly about each aspect of the circle.

Belonging

There are two important things to remember about belonging. First, the most significant groups to which we belong are the smallest, the ones in which we play the clearest roles, the ones in which relationships are closest and most intimate. This is why family is so important and why those without blood kin to whom they feel they belong need surrogate families. This is why small classes and schools, special classes, and professional specialties with distinctive concerns and methods are more attractive for many than the larger, more amorphous or ambiguously defined groups. Second, a sense of belonging is based on perceived similarities or commonalities, not differences or diversities. To the extent that we see that sameness overshadows difference among us, we feel belonging; to the extent that we believe difference overshadows sameness in our group, we feel that we do not belong. This is why I have such hope that we will see multicultural education as something that emphasizes commonality more than diversity.

Mastery

We know that the children we are concerned about really need to feel a sense of achievement; to perceive that they are making progress in learning important and useful skills; to see the world as a stable, predictable, understandable place. It should come as no surprise that we adults who work with these children have the same need, that our emotional well-being and professional behavior will be enhanced by our mastery. What undermines the achievement of mastery? I suggest that mastery is undermined by anything that makes the world unnecessarily complex, unpredictable, or not understandable, including the notion that you cannot really know anything or make progress. But think about how many of our students believe this—see the world as unknowable and unpredictable, as chaotic. The postmodern view undermines the very sense of mastery and predictability that we need for ourselves and our students.

Independence

Independence does not mean isolation or lack of connection or belonging. But it does mean that there are important things we can do regardless of the actions of others. This is what we call *autonomy*. Reformers who say that the improvement of special education depends on the reform of general education undermine our need for independence. As I have suggested elsewhere, we need to focus on what we can change, what we can do as special educators to improve the education of students with disabilities regardless of the direction general education takes. Again, this does not mean that we fail to recognize the importance of general education and its improvement, but simply that we know to what professional group we belong most clearly, that we master the tasks of special educators, and then act as independently or autonomously as necessary to accomplish our purposes.

Generosity

Generosity does not just mean giving stuff to others; it means being generous enough in spirit to endure slights or offenses without retaliation. It means developing empathy and a forgiving spirit. It means abandoning the desire for payback or getback. I have spoken and written previously about civility in our culture and in our schools (Kauffman & Burbach, 1997), mentioning the group offense patrol and the slight-trigger disease. Group offense patrol (GOP) means that you have your antennae out for any possible offense of your group. Slight-trigger disease (STD) means that the smallest perceived slight will trigger in you a reaction to get back, pay back, cost the other person, make the other person suffer. Generosity of spirit means being slow to anger toward other people because we have a sense of humor about ourselves and can practice self-restraint.

The "Car Talk" Model of Special Education

6

I'm going to end by proposing something I hope readers will not find outrageous or upsetting: the "Car Talk" model of special education. I listen sometimes to a program on National Public Radio called "Car Talk." "Car Talk" is also a feature in some newspapers, and it has a Web site at www.cartalk.org. Two mechanics, the Magliozzi brothers, Tom and Ray—who call themselves Click and Clack, the Tappet brothers—host the show. They take calls from people who are having car trouble or want advice about cars or car repair. They are consummate mechanics. They know the science and technology of cars. They love to solve puzzles and problems, which is to say they are scientists. But they are also very funny, full of good humor, including joking with people about their problems and making self-deprecating wisecracks.

Now, I understand that children are not cars, that our business is dealing with people, not machines, and that a totally mechanistic view of our work is not appropriate. But I think there are lessons to be learned from the Magliozzi brothers, that there are some valid parallels between their work and ours, and that a significant part of what we do—a significant part, not everything—involves helping people find solutions to problems. And, as I indicated earlier, I think an empirical, scientific approach to these problems often provides the best solution—the one that our clients find most reliable, useful, cost-effective, and satisfying. So, although I realize that children are not cars, I think "Car Talk" can be said to reflect the Circle of Courage. Here's how:

- *Belonging*—Click and Clack clearly and proudly identify themselves as mechanics. They belong to that group, and they are proud of it.

- *Mastery*—Click and Clack know their stuff and are able to discriminate problems they can solve from those that are simply preferences on the part of their clients. They are scientific problem solvers who understand the value and limitations of science and its alternatives.

- *Independence*—Click and Clack do not see themselves as able to function properly only if the car manufacturing industry and the auto sales industry are restructured or reformed. They are in the business of car maintenance and repair, which will always provide a needed function. And they will do it well regardless of what happens in the rest of the auto industry.

- *Generosity*—The Magliozzi brothers are not so serious about themselves or their work that they cannot see the humor in what they do, either as individuals or as mechanics. They have a lot of fun because they are so comfortable with who they are, they are masters of their trade, and they know how to help others. We could do no better than to strive to be like them in their achievement of the Circle of Courage.

My hope is that as we enter the new millennium we will be proud to belong to special education, achieve mastery of our science and craft, act autonomously, and increase our generosity of spirit. If we do, then we will make our own lives and the lives of the children and families we serve significantly better.

References

American Association for Employment in Education. (1998). *Job search handbook for educators.* Evanston, IL: Author.

Bower, E. (1969). *Early identification of emotionally handicapped children in school* (2nd ed.). Springfield, IL: Thomas.

Brendtro, L. K., & Brokenleg, M. (1993). Beyond the curriculum of control. *Journal of Emotional and Behavioral Problems, 1*(4), 5–11.

Cooley, S. (1995). *Suspension/expulsion of regular and special education students in Kansas.* Topeka: Kansas State Board of Education.

Costenbader, V., & Buntaine, R. (1999). Diagnostic discrimination between social maladjustment and emotional disturbance: An empirical study. *Journal of Emotional and Behavioral Disorders, 7,* 2–10.

Fagen, S., Long, N., & Stevens, D. (1975). *Teaching children self-control.* Columbus, OH: Merrill.

Goodman, E. (1999, March 26). Computer games for girls maintain old stereotypes. *The Charlottesville Daily Progress,* A8.

Gould, S. J. (1997). *Questioning the millennium. A rationalist's guide to a precisely arbitrary countdown.* New York: Harmony.

Haring, N., & Phillips, E. (1962). *Educating emotionally disturbed children.* New York: McGraw-Hill.

Hewett, F. (1968). *The emotionally disturbed child in the classroom.* Boston: Allyn & Bacon.

Hobbs, N. (1964). *Project Re-ED.* Nashville, TN: George Peabody College for Teachers.

Hobbs, N. (1975). *The futures of children.* San Francisco: Jossey-Bass.

Kauffman, J. M. (1997). *Characteristics of emotional and behavioral disorders of children and youth* (6th ed.). Upper Saddle River, NJ: Prentice-Hall.

Kauffman, J. M. (1999a). Commentary: Today's special education and its messages for tomorrow. *The Journal of Special Education, 32,* 244–254.

Kauffman, J. M. (in press a). How we prevent the prevention of emotional and behavioral disorders. *Exceptional Children.*

Kauffman, J. M. (in press b). The role of science in behavioral disorders. *Behavioral Disorders.*

Kauffman, J. M., & Burbach, H. J. (1997). On creating a climate of classroom civility. *Phi Delta Kappan, 79,* 320–325.

Kelly, E. (1990). *Differential test of conduct and emotional problems.* East Aurora, NY: Slosson.

Knitzer, J., Steinberg, Z., & Fleisch, B. (1990). *At the schoolhouse door.* New York: Bank Street College of Education.

Long, N. (1974). Nicholas J. Long. In J. Kauffman & C. Lewis (Eds.), *Teaching children with behavior disorders: Personal perspectives* (pp. 168–196). Columbus, OH: Merrill.

Long, N., Morse, W., & Newman, R. (Eds.). (1996). *Conflict in the classroom* (5th ed.). Austin, TX: Pro-Ed.

Mackie, R., & Dunn, L. (1954). *College and university programs for the preparation of teachers of exceptional children.* (DHEW/OE Bulletin No. 13). Washington, DC: U.S. Government Printing Office.

Morse, W. (1965). The crisis teacher. In N. Long, W. Morse, & R. Newman (Eds.) *Conflict in the classroom* (pp. 251–254). Belmont, CA: Wadworth.

Morse, W., Cutler, R., & Fink, A. (1964). *Public school classes for the emotionally handicapped: A research analysis.* Reston, VA: The Council for Exceptional Children.

Naslund, S. (1987). Life space interviewing: A psychoeducational intervention model for teaching pupil insight and measuring program effectiveness. *The Pointer, 31*(2) 12–15.

National Commission on Teaching and America's Future. (1996). *What matters most: Teaching for America's future.* New York: Author.

Olson, P., Freeman, L., Bowman, J., & Pieper, J. (1972). *The university can't train teachers.* Lincoln: University of Nebraska.

Quay, H., & Werry, J. (Eds.). (1986). *Psychopathological disorders of childhood* (3rd ed.). New York: Wiley.

Raspberry, W. (1999, April 12). An end to our American argot? The *Charlottesville Daily Progress,* A23.

Redl, F., & Wineman, D. (1957). *The aggressive child.* New York: Free Press.

Rhodes, W. (1972). *A study of child variance* (Vol. 1). Ann Arbor: University of Michigan Press.

Robins, L. (1966). *Deviant children grown up.* Baltimore: Williams & Wilkins.

Simpson, R., Whelan, R., & Zabel, R. (1993). Special education personnel preparation in the 21st century: Issues and strategies. *Remedial and Special Education, 14*(2), 7–22.

Skinner, B. (1953). *Science and human behavior.* New York: Macmillan.

Sylvester, C. (1909). *Journeys through bookland.* Chicago: Thompson.

Tompkins, J. (1969). An analysis: Needs, progress and issues in the preparation of personnel in the education of emotionally disturbed children. *The Journal of Special Education, 3*(1), 101–111.

U.S. Department of Education. (1995). *Seventeenth annual report to Congress on the implementation of the Individuals with Disabilities Education Act.* Washington, DC: Author.

U.S. Department of Health, Education, and Welfare. (1954). *Statistics of special education for exceptional children, 1952–53.* (DHEW Chapter 5). Washington, DC: U.S. Government Printing Office.

U.S. General Accounting Office. (1995). *Report on crime.* Washington, DC: U.S. Government Printing Office.

Whelan, R. (1991). Developing standards for special education teacher certification: Process and product. In R. Rutherford, C. Nelson, & S. Forness (Eds.), *Basis of severe behavioral disorders in children and youth* (pp. 339–354). Boston: College-Hill.

Whelan, R. (1998). *Emotional and behavior disorders: A 25 year focus.* Denver: Love.

Zabel, R. (1988). Preparation of teachers for behaviorally disordered students. In M. Wang, M. Reynolds, & H. Walberg (Eds.), *Handbook of special education research and practice* (Vol. 2, pp. 171–194). New York: Pergamon.

Don't Miss CCBD's Second Mini-Library Series

Mini-Library Series on Successful Interventions for the 21st Century

Edited by Lyndal M. Bullock and Robert A. Gable
#D5245   1997 $72   CEC Members $50.40
Separate titles: $11.40 each   CEC Members $8

24-Hour Fax 703-264-9494

Alternative Programs for Students with Social, Emotional, or Behavioral Problems
Mary Magee Quinn and Robert B. Rutherford, Jr.
#D5238   49pp   0-86586-304-0

Curriculum and Instruction Practices for Students with Emotional/ Behavioral Disorders
Edited by Rex E. Schmid and William Evans
#D5239   58pp   ISBN 0-86586-305-0

Developing Personal and Interpersonal Responsibility in Children and Youth with Emotional/Behavioral Disorders
Sylvia Rockwell, Santa Cuccio, Beth Kirtley, and Gwen Smith
#D5240   41pp   ISBN 0-86586-306-7

Developing Social Competence in Children and Youth with Challenging Behaviors
Kristine J. Melloy, Carol A. Davis, Joseph H. Wehby, Francie R. Murry, and Jennifer Leiber
#D5241   42pp   ISBN 0-86586-307-5

Enhancing Self-Respect: A Challenge for Teachers of Students with Emotional/ Behavioral Disorders
Ann Fitzsimons-Lovett
#D5242   40pp   ISBN 0-86586-308-3

Individual and Systemic Approaches to Collaboration and Consultation on Behalf of Students with Emotional/ Behavioral Disorders
Robert A. Gable, George Sugai, Tim Lewis, J. Ron Nelson, Douglas Cheney, Stephan P. Safran, and Joan S. Safran
#D5243   45pp   ISBN 0-86586-309-1

Teaching Children and Youth Self-Control: Applications of Perceptual Control Theory
John W. Maag
#D5244   42pp   ISBN 0-86586-310-5

From the Retrospective Series on Critical Issues in Emotional/Behavioral Disorders . . .

Improving the Social Skills of Children and Youth with Emotional/Behavioral Disorders

Series Editors: Lyndal M. Bullock, Robert A. Gable, and Robert B. Rutherford, Jr.

Topics include various approaches to enhancing and maintaining social skills, including self-monitoring, "entrapment" (control of behavior by naturally occurring reinforcements), peer mediation, problem-solving, peer confrontation, and structured learning.

#D5158   1996   120pp   ISBN 0-86586-283-4

Preparation of Teachers of Students with Emotional/ Behavioral Disorders

Lyndal M. Bullock, Robert A. Gable, and Robert B. Rutherford, Jr.

This volume focuses on the challenges of preparing teachers to work with children with emotional/behavioral disorders. The editors have included articles which represent the diverse opinions and directions of current training. Topics also include intervention research, inclusion, classroom-based programs, and the needs of inner city pupils.

#D5279   1998   122pp   ISBN 0-86586-321-0